Super Women in Science

THE WOMEN'S HALL OF FAME SERIES

SUPER WOMEN IN SCIENCE

BY KELLY DI DOMENICO

Second Story Press

NATIONAL LIBRARY OF CANADA CATALOGUING IN PUBLICATION

Di Domenico, Kelly, 1977-
Super women in science / Kelly Di Domenico.

(Women's hall of fame series)
Includes bibliographical references.
ISBN 1-896764-66-5

1. Women scientists--Biography--Juvenile literature.
I. Title. II. Series.

Q141.D54 2002   j509'.2'2   C2002-904273-9

Edited by Laura McCurdy, Frances Rooney and Rhea Tregebov
Designed by Laura McCurdy

Printed and bound in Canada

Second Story Press gratefully acknowledges the support of the Ontario Arts Council and the Canada Council for the Arts for our publishing program. We acknowledge the financial support of the Government of Canada through the Book Publishing Industry Development Program, and the Government of Ontario through the Tax Credit Program.

 Canada Council   Conseil des Arts
for the Arts   du Canada

Published by
SECOND STORY PRESS
720 Bathurst Street, Suite 301
Toronto, Ontario
M5S 2R4

www.secondstorypress.on.ca

TABLE OF CONTENTS

For my parents

INTRODUCTION

Faye Ajzenborg-Selove quietly made her way through the dark hallway that led to the laboratory. Her friends had made sure that the door to the laboratory would be unlocked so she wouldn't have a problem getting in. After working on her experiment in nuclear physics through part of the night, she carefully made sure everything was in its original place when she left. It was crucial not to arouse any suspicion.

The reason for this covert operation was not because of some top-secret experiment Faye was working on. Rather, it was all because she was a woman, and Princeton University was very clear about one thing: no women at the school. So Faye was forced to sneak in at night to use the equipment in the laboratory.

This may seem strange, but when Faye was working as a scientist in the 1950s, women were not welcome in the world of science. It was not unusual for a woman to have to go to the extraordinary lengths that Faye did simply to practice what they loved and make a contribution to knowledge.

We have been taught that science was traditionally the domain of men and we sometimes have a hard time naming female scientists. But the truth is that women have always been involved in science.

In ancient China, the empress Shi Dun worked with one of her servants to make the first paper out of the bark of the mulberry tree. In the Middle Ages, Celia Grillo Borromeo was so well known in her home town of Genoa, Italy, for her scientific knowledge that the city put her on a coin. In the 18th century, Caroline Herschel became one of the first paid female scientists when King George III of England awarded her a pension for discovering eight new comets.

Being paid has been very rare, though. Most women throughout history have had to practice science as a hobby because universities would not accept them as students and the scientific community refused to accept them as professionals. Hedy Lamarr was a well-known movie star in the 1930s, but few people know that she also helped to develop satellite communications, which is what makes cellular phones work. This was also the case of Lady Ada Byron Lovelace, who helped design the first known computer. As a proper Victorian lady she could not work, but her interest in science was too strong for her to ignore, so she did what she could and others got the credit.

Imagine trying to be a scientist during the 19th century, when men were even trying to use science to prove that women were inferior. They said that because a woman's brain is shaped differently than a man's, she must be less intelligent. Well, Marie Curie was a scientist at that time and her work with radioactivity earned her two Nobel prizes!

The attitude that women were not smart enough to be scientists prevailed for a long time, but many women simply ignored it. They were curious about the world around them and wanted to play a part in discovering and understanding all its wonders.

The impact of women in science is all around us. If you look at your periodic table of the elements in science class, you will notice that the element meitnerium is named for the scientist Lise Meitner. The drug that makes organ transplants possible was developed by Gertrude Belle Elion. And when a police officer survives a gunshot to the chest, it is thanks to Stephanie Kwolek, who invented Kevlar, the material used in bullet-proof vests.

Today there are many different fields of study in the scientific world. As new areas of research have sprung up, women have risen to the challenge. Hypatia was a brilliant scholar who taught early astronomical theories as well as mathematics and philosophy. Rosalind Franklin helped with one of the biggest discoveries in the field of genetics, and Rachel Carson brought the relatively unknown field of ecology to a wider audience with her writing. Harriet Brooks Pitcher and Maria Goeppert-Mayer made their mark in different areas of physics. Mary Anning was a pioneer in the study of fossils, or what is now called paleontology. Catherine Hickson studies volcanoes around the world. Biruté Galdikas spends several months of every year in the rainforests of Borneo as one of the first people to attempt a long-term observation of orangutans.

Other trailblazing women in science faced discrimination not only as women, but as people of color. Chien-Shiung Wu had to work extra hard to prove herself in the field of physics because of wartime distrust of people from Asia. Despite the doubts of her teachers, Mae Jemison earned both an engineering degree and a medical degree, and became the first African-American woman astronaut.

All the women in the book share such qualities as persistence and dedication. No matter what they were told — *we won't hire you, you can't do that* — they just didn't listen because they loved their work so much.

Today they are recognized not just as remarkable women, but also as remarkable scientists. The lesson to be learned from all of them is that if you pursue what you love, and are confident in yourself, you can overcome the odds.

1

HYPATIA

355–415

Synesius, a young Roman student, loved learning and often went to the outdoor amphitheater in the center of Cyrene, a city in what is today Libya, to see plays. But when it seemed he had learned all he could from the teachers in Cyrene, he set sail for Alexandria in Egypt to study with the best teacher in the empire. What a privilege it was to be accepted as one of the pupils of Hypatia!

Hypatia was born in Alexandria around 355 A.D. This magnificent city played an important role in her life. It was founded in 331 B.C. by the famous Greek conqueror, Alexander the Great, to celebrate his victories and the cultural tradition of Greece.

The people of Greece were known for their curiosity about the world and their desire to understand it. Their thoughts about where they came from and what it meant to be human came to be known as *philosophy*. They also made important observations about the natural world. When they looked up at the night sky, they realized they were gazing at stars and other planets. And they recognized that the three angles of any triangle always add up to 180 degrees. The Greeks were creating mathematics and science! At that time, though, philosophy, math and science were not seen as separate subjects. Wondering about life and the world involved all three subjects.

Alexander made sure that Alexandria would inspire more great thinking by building the biggest library in the world there. As a consequence, the city attracted some of the brightest minds of the Greek world. By the time Hypatia was born, over six centuries after its founding, Alexandria was part of the powerful Roman Empire. People from many cultures and religions lived there, and the Greek community continued to uphold and contribute to their rich culture. Hypatia was descended from the noble and educated Greek people that had settled in the city during the time of Alexander. Her father, Theon, was a scholar who taught at The Museum, a school in Alexandria that was much like a university and was affiliated with the famous library. Theon taught his daughter everything he knew and she quickly developed her own love for learning.

Founded in the fourth century B.C., the famous library at Alexandria was built to house all the writings in existence at that time. Within a century it held over 700,000 manuscripts. It became an important cultural center and had a school attached to it. It is believed that the library was burned in a fire that swept through Alexandria in the fifth century A.D.

12

Always an eager student, Hypatia convinced her father to send her to Greece so she could continue her studies in Athens, where so many of the thinkers she admired came from. It was very rare for a woman to be accepted into a school, but Hypatia's brilliant mind was so impressive that the men could find no reason to keep her out. In fact, Hypatia did so well at the school in Athens that they awarded her a crown of laurels — an honor given only to the best students.

When she returned to Alexandria, Hypatia had surpassed her father in her studies. She was now ready to teach others. Knowledge was considered sacred and only the wisest could become teachers. Few were more intelligent or devoted to the pursuit of knowledge than Hypatia, who once said: "Reserve your right to think, for even to think wrongly is better than not to think at all."

Hypatia began to teach a small group of students at her home, giving them lively lectures about math and astronomy and having philosophical debates with them. Hypatia was strict but her students loved her and her teaching. Her fame grew and students like Synesius traveled to Alexandria from all over the Roman Empire to study with her.

As a teacher, Hypatia also wrote commentaries, which were almost like textbooks, explaining the mathematical theories of some of the great thinkers of ancient Greece. These writings dealt mostly with the same kind of geometry and algebra that we learn today.

Hypatia always continued to learn. She knew a great deal about astronomy (the study of the universe), and with Synesius built one of the first *astrolabes*. This instrument had originally been designed around 150 B.C., but it was a long time before one was actually built and astrolabes were still very rare in Hypatia's time. An astrolabe was made of several plates that rotated so that the latitude of the sun and the stars could be measured. These measurements then allowed a person to know when the sun would rise and set, as well as the time of day. The astrolabe eventually became an important tool for sailors, who could tell where they were by reading the stars with it.

According to letters Synesius wrote, Hypatia was interested in other devices for exploring the world. She also built a *hydroscope*, which is used to see below the surface of water.

Hypatia had become the leading intellectual in Alexandria and its citizens greatly admired her. When she rode in her chariot along the streets of the city, people would throw her flowers. They had never known anyone so dedicated to learning. She was described as being even more beautiful than Cleopatra and many men asked for her hand in marriage. But Hypatia refused them all, fearing that marriage would interfere with her teaching and studying.

When Hypatia gave public lectures, Alexandrians would cram themselves into the public hall to hear what this striking woman draped in her flowing white robe had to say. Sometimes she talked about astronomy, other times about philosophy or math. Many people found that the ideas that Hypatia shared enlightened their lives, and those who got to see her felt very honored.

Alexandria began to experience political upheaval at that time, and as much as Hypatia tried to lead a peaceful life of study, she was affected by what was going on. The Romans had recently converted to Christianity and were encouraging people within the empire to do the same. Many refused, since they still believed in a religion of many gods they thought controlled the different elements, such as water or love. But a new bishop, Cyril, had arrived in

Alexandria, and he felt that he could convert most of the city's people.

Hypatia was not a Christian, yet she was not opposed to Christianity. She openly welcomed anyone to study with her as long as they were committed and showed high intellectual abilities, and several of her students were Christian. Bishop Cyril, though, saw her as an obstacle to his goal. He believed that as long as people were interested in Hypatia and her teachings they would not be interested in Christianity.

The situation worsened when the emperor of Rome sent a new government official, Orestes, to make sure that Alexandria ran properly. He had heard of Hypatia before arriving in the city, and wanted to meet this remarkable woman. He was impressed by her wisdom, and as time went on he began to consult her about decisions he had to make concerning the city. Hypatia and Orestes respected each other and she supported him. This enraged Cyril

Hypatia's astrolabe has been lost, but this one, built in France around 1300, uses the same principles.

and he became jealous of Hypatia. He wanted to be the one who advised Orestes.

Cyril began to spread rumors about Hypatia. How could a woman know so much? Why was she able to predict eclipses and understand the stars? She must be a witch! Cyril said that she was casting spells on the important people of Alexandria so they would listen only to her. Unfortunately, many people in Alexandria were not well educated and they believed Cyril.

One day, while riding home, Hypatia was accosted by

an angry mob. The crowd pulled her out of her chariot and dragged her to a church, where she was murdered. The year was 415, and Hypatia's horrific death signaled the end of the intellectual spirit that had inspired the birth of the great city of Alexandria. Not long after, the great library was destroyed and the city fell into a centuries-long period when learning ceased to be important.

Hypatia's tragic death sometimes overshadows her achievements. She had become the leading thinker of her time, famous in Alexandria and across an entire empire. She continues to inspire us today because she continued to strive to understand the world by studying it even after it became dangerous to do so.

2

MARY ANNING

1799–1847

According to legend, as a young girl Mary Anning encountered a dragon while walking along the pebbled beach of Lyme Regis, England. That's not quite what happened, but Mary's is a great story and a remarkable one.

Mary Anning was actually a fossil-hunter, or what today we would call a paleontologist. She lived at a time when very few people had any idea what a fossil was or even that prehistoric creatures like dinosaurs had ever existed. Her hard work and determination contributed to our understanding of these ancient, now extinct creatures.

Little is known about the early part of Mary's life. One story says that a thunderstorm once broke out while Mary, who was only a year old, was being cared for by a local woman. They took shelter under a tree with some other people, Mary bundled in blankets and huddled in the woman's arms. A huge bolt of lightning struck the tree, and Mary, it is told, was the only one to survive the electrical shock.

Whether or not that story is true, we do know that Mary grew up in the small coastal town of Lyme Regis, in southern England. Buried in the steep cliffs along the shore of Lyme Regis were mysterious creatures — overgrown crocodiles with large piercing teeth and lizards with wings and long pointed beaks — which would provide Mary's income and her place in the history of science.

Mary's parents had moved to Lyme Regis so her father, a carpenter, could find employment. He worked hard but still struggled to provide for his family. One day, while strolling along the stony beach, he came across some rocks that had designs in them. When he looked at the rocks more closely, he realized that the designs were actually the outlines of small creatures. He had stumbled across a shoreline filled with *fossils*.

Paleontology is the study of the forms of life existing in prehistoric times, as they are known from fossil remains of animals and plants.

Fossils are created when an animal or plant gets buried over time under layers and layers of rock and soil. Eventually the bones or plant matter decays and the mold that has been left in the sediment is filled in with minerals and hardens into a fossil. Fossils are important because they can tell us about animals and plants that existed millions of years ago. They provide us with information about the earth's past and suggest what the earth must have once been like.

The fossils of Lyme Regis show that the town site was once covered in water. As the seas receded, the creatures living in the water died and gradually became encased under the layers and rocks that now form the deep ridges of the landscape along the shore. Most of the fossils that Mary's father discovered were of *ammonites*, small creatures that looked like miniature snakes lying in a swirled position.

The Philpot Museum in the coastal town of Lyme Regis is a history museum that includes a special section on Mary and the fossils found in the town. The museum is built on the site where the house Mary was born in stood.

It was a good time for fossil-hunting. Many English nobles were taking a keen interest in science. Fossils were being found in different parts of England and many people collected them as "curios" (short for curiosities). Since Mary's father was still having trouble earning enough to support the family, he decided to collect fossils and sell them to tourists. Fossil-hunting became a part-time business for him and he quickly became an expert at it. He often took Mary along with him to the beach, and before long the intelligent little girl could find fossils on her own.

In 1810, tragedy struck the family. Mary's father died. The responsibility for supporting the family fell on eleven-year-old Mary and her younger brother, Joseph. They decided to take over their father's business of collecting and selling fossils.

Only a few months later, Joseph came across the imprint of a head that appeared to have belonged to a very large and unfamiliar creature. Mary was fascinated by the size of the fossil, and wondered what sort of animal could have possessed such a massive head. Mary immediately knew that this mysterious find was an important one. She was curious to see the full skeleton, so she patiently continued to search for the missing pieces.

Mary scoured the shores of Lyme Regis. The best time to search for fossils is after the tide has come in, when the forceful waves may have knocked rock fragments from the jagged cliffs above the beach. The tide often loosened the rocks, and fossils became exposed. Every day, Mary faced the risk of being hit by falling rocks as she searched for fossils. She also sometimes rushed out during rainstorms to see if the pounding rain had caused any rock avalanches.

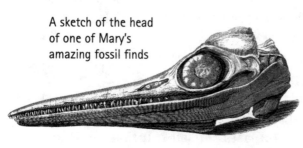

A sketch of the head of one of Mary's amazing fossil finds

It took Mary a year to find the rest of the fossil. She assembled the pieces like a jigsaw puzzle, and what emerged was a very strange animal. It looked like a reptile since it had a long crocodile snout, yet it also had some of the features of a fish, such as fins for swimming. Strangest of all, it was much larger than any lizard or fish Mary had ever seen, over five meters long (nearly seventeen feet), or about the length of two modern cars!

The local newspapers quickly took notice of Mary's incredible discovery and wrote many stories about the young girl who had unearthed a monster. Word spread quickly about the fossil and much excitement was created among scientists in England. The fossil was sold to a private collector who eventually passed it on to the Natural History Museum in London. In 1817, the extinct half-fish, half-lizard creature was given the name *ichthyosaur*, meaning lizard of the sea. By the time the fossil was named and recognized as an important scientific discovery, people had forgotten that it was Mary Anning who had found it.

As she grew older, Mary became the main fossil gatherer in the family. She supplied specimens to a growing number of fossil collectors, one of whom, Lieutenant-Colonel Thomas Jane Birch, bought most of his collection from her. As Birch got to know the Anning family, he realized that despite Mary's remarkable work, they still had financial problems. He decided to help by auctioning his entire collection and giving the Annings all the proceeds.

The event, held in 1820, drew large crowds, all wanting to see Mary's mysterious discoveries. The auction also gave her some of the recognition she deserved for her work. Normally, when fossils were donated to museums, the name of the giver and not the discoverer was attached to the specimen. Finally, people were realizing that it was Mary who had uncovered all these fascinating fossils.

Despite the auction, though, Mary's work was still generally overlooked. This was the case with one of her greatest discoveries. Birch's collection included a headless skeleton that Mary had found. The enormous skeleton had an oval body with a long, giraffe-like neck. Two men bought the creature and presented it to the Geological Society in London. The fossil was accepted and named *plesiosaur*, but there was no mention of Mary's role in the discovery. In fact, the Geological Society, an organization that was founded in 1807 to bring together those interested in the study of rocks and minerals, never accepted Mary as one of its members because she was a woman.

The Geological Society of London did not admit women until 1904 — 57 years after Mary died!

Frustratingly, Mary was never viewed as a true scientist

either, because she was a working-class woman who had received little education. British scientists tended to see Mary as a mere collector and seller of fossils, like so many of the other residents of Lyme Regis who set up stalls along the streets. What distinguished Mary from the rest, however, was her extensive knowledge and her sharp eye for recognizing fossils that were extraordinary and significant. She tried not to be discouraged by the fact that she received so little credit. Instead she focused her energy on learning as much as she could about geology. She read many books on the subject and spoke as often as she could with others who shared her interest.

Her keen knowledge did not go completely unnoticed. Lady Harriet Silvester, an English noblewoman who met Mary, remarked that "The extraordinary thing in this young woman is that she has made herself so thoroughly acquainted with the science that the moment she finds any

Women in the world of paleontology

Zofia Kielan-Jaworowska, a Polish paleontologist, led extremely successful expeditions to the Gobi desert from 1963 to 1971. She unearthed fossils of many different kinds of dinosaurs, and in 1971 she made one of the most remarkable discoveries yet — fossil remains of a protoceratops and a velociraptor caught in a deadly struggle.

In 2001, Catherine Forster and her research team discovered the remains of a new dinosaur in Madagascar, Africa. Named makiasaur, this carnivore was about the size of a German shepherd dog.

Mary Dawson is Curator of Vertebrate Paleontology at the Carnegie Museum of Natural History in Washington, D.C., a position she was once told would never be held by a woman!

bones she knows to what tribe they belong. That this poor, ignorant girl should be so blessed, for by reading and application she has arrived to that degree of knowledge as to be in the habit of writing and talking with professors and other clever men on the subject, and they all acknowledge that she understands more of the science than anyone else in this kingdom."

Mary never let the fact that she was not accepted into the scientific community stop her from doing the work that she loved. The townspeople of Lyme Regis were accustomed to seeing her roaming the beach accompanied by her dog, a little hammer for digging in the rocks in one hand and a small basket to carry her treasures in the other.

Through her diligence, Mary continued to make important and amazing discoveries. In 1828, she found a *pterodactyl macronyx,* a sort of flying reptile, and in 1829, she came across a fish fossil named *squaloraja.* That year, Mary also traveled to London for the first time. She visited the Geological Society and the British Museum, where she must have felt a huge surge of pride when she came to a glass case where some of her fossils were displayed.

Around 1838, Mary grew too weak to keep up with the physical demands of her work and reluctantly retired from fossil hunting. But her work continued to have an enormous impact on life in Victorian England. At the time, it was generally believed that the earth was only 6000 years old, but Mary's fossils caused scientists to question whether the earth was actually much older. In fact, today we know that the creatures Mary unearthed lived during what is called the *Jurassic period,* over 140 million years ago.

Mary did live to see the introduction of the term "dinosaur." A scientist named Richard Owen recognized that fossils like the ones Mary had found were not actually reptiles or fish, but must belong to a new species, one he named *Dinosauria*, meaning terrible lizards.

Mary was more than the young girl who encountered a fossilized dragon, more than the poor woman who sold rocks with shapes in them to support her family. As one of the first paleontologists, Mary came face to face with our prehistoric past and recognized that fabulous creatures had lived in it.

3

HARRIET BROOKS PITCHER

1876-1933

When we hear the term pioneer, we often think of people heading into the west in covered wagons to settle new land. Harriet Brooks, who was born during the time of these pioneers, became quite a different kind of pioneer. Harriet ventured into the new territory of *radioactivity*, an area of science that explores the *atom*. Her discoveries would help provide a foundation for understanding radioactivity and its many uses, including treating cancer and taking x-rays.

Harriet Brooks was born July 2, 1876 in Exeter, Ontario. There were nine children in the family, and Harriet was particularly close to her two sisters, Edith and

25

Elizabeth. Life was much different then. People worked very hard, and Harriet helped with chores like taking coal into the house to burn for heat, sewing clothes, and making preserves and bread. On top of all these duties, she managed to do very well in school.

In high school, she and Elizabeth were both interested in science. The two sisters must have discussed what they learned, encouraging each other and asking questions. After school they would sometimes walk a few kilometers (about a mile and a half) to the library, where they explored the books to see what else the world of science could reveal to them.

As high school came to an end, the sisters decided that they wanted to go to university, a very unusual choice for girls at that time. For Harriet and Elizabeth, this decision was even more remarkable since their parents could not afford to send them to university and did not encourage them to further their education. But the sisters were ready to go down that path, even without much support.

Harriet applied to McGill University in Montreal, Quebec. She was accepted, granted a scholarship, and off she went! Two years later, Elizabeth would follow.

In 1894, Harriet was one of only a handful of female students at McGill. It was an uncomfortable situation, since some people didn't want her there because she was a woman. McGill had only issued a degree to a woman for the first time in 1888, and according

Students at university first complete a bachelor's degree, which takes three or four years. If they find an area of study they really like, they might do a more specialized master's degree, and then a Doctorate of Philosophy or a Ph.D. These last two degrees involve a lot of research, and writing a long essay called a thesis or a dissertation. Once you have a Ph.D. you become a "doctor," but you don't have to wear a stethoscope!

to Canadian law women were not even "persons"! Even though some of the male students on campus were rude to Harriet, staring at her or pointing and laughing as she walked down the hallways to her classes, she was determined to stay. She had a resilient spirit, and her keen mind impressed both her professors and her peers. By her third year she was elected class president, and in 1898 she graduated with first-rank honors in mathematics and a teaching diploma to ensure that she could get a job. Harriet was not eager to teach, though. She wanted to work where the real magic took place, as a researcher in a laboratory.

While Harriet was approaching graduation and struggling to decide what to do next, a famous physicist arrived at McGill. Ernest Rutherford was from New Zealand and had an international reputation. He had been working at the Cavendish Laboratory at Cambridge University in England, but was attracted to McGill because of its new state-of-the-art laboratory and collection of scientific equipment. These resources meant Rutherford could conduct highly sophisticated experiments.

Rutherford wanted the brightest people to be on his research team, and he picked Harriet as his first graduate student. She was excited about having the chance to work toward a master's degree while delving into the mysterious world of radioactivity.

When Harriet began working with Rutherford,

Members of the McGill University physics department, about 1899. Harriet is at the back, and Rutherford is the farthest right.

radioactivity was just being discovered. In 1895, a scientist named Wilhelm Roentgen had learned that the imprint of the bones of a hand would appear on a piece of photographic paper when certain rays were directed at the hand as it lay on the paper. In other words, the rays could pass through flesh but not bone. But what were these rays and where exactly did they come from? A year later, Henri Becquerel discovered that the element uranium produced such rays. In France, Marie Curie studied these rays. She called them radioactive, since radio is the Latin word for ray. After many tests, she startled other scientists by claiming that radioactivity is a basic property of certain elements.

Dmitry Mendeleyev began compiling the periodic table of elements in 1869. At that time, there were only 63 known elements and Mendeleyev organized them into a chart using their masses. He noticed patterns and was able to predict that others would be discovered. Today there are 118 elements on the periodic table.

The world is made up of the various chemical *elements*. The elements hydrogen and oxygen, for example, make water. Each element has its own characteristics, such as weight and density, and each comes in the form of a distinct *atom*. At that time scientists believed that atoms were the smallest particle that existed, that they could not be divided into smaller parts, and that they never changed. But Marie Curie was suggesting that something inside the atom does change to create these rays. At around the same time, the British scientist J.J. Thomson discovered that smaller parts (*electrons*) do exist inside the atom. The basic understanding of science was being overturned, and Harriet was about to enter a broad new landscape of scientific discovery.

Rutherford had earlier observed that as well as rays, radioactive elements also released some kind of substance,

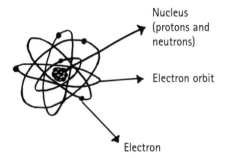

RUTHERFORD'S MODEL OF THE ATOM. Rutherford created this model of the atom, with electrons orbiting a central core, called a nucleus. Now we know that there are two types of particles in the nucleus, protons and neutrons.

Nucleus (protons and neutrons)

Electron orbit

Electron

which he called an *emanation*. He did not really know what this emanation was, so he put Harriet in charge of studying it. Until that point, it had been believed that anything that was emitted from a radioactive element would have the same properties as that element. But Harriet found that the emanation was actually a gas that had a different weight from the element that was producing it. She and Rutherford realized that this meant a *transmutation* was taking place, that one element was transforming into another (today this process is known as radioactive decay). The emanation was in fact an entirely new element — they had just discovered *radon*.

Through her work with Rutherford, Harriet became the first woman to earn a master's degree in physics from McGill. In 1901 she went to Bryn Mawr, a leading women's college in Pennsylvania, to further her studies. After one year there, Harriet won the European Fellowship, a prestigious scholarship that allowed her to study at Cambridge University in England for a year. Just before her departure, Harriet learned the exciting news that she would be working with a research group led by J.J. Thomson!

At Cambridge, Harriet continued to work on radioactive elements. But the atmosphere there was different, and Harriet missed the respect and support Rutherford had given her. He had treated her as an equal and made sure that she received full credit for her contributions.

After a year, Harriet decided to return to Montreal. Back in the familiar environment of McGill, she rejoined Rutherford's team. Her experiments were critical in the discovery that radioactive elements go through several changes over time, another important step in understanding radioactivity.

In 1904, Harriet left McGill to take a teaching position at Barnard College, the women's college of Columbia University in New York City. Perhaps she was feeling the pressures and limitations of being a female scientist — it was unlikely that she would ever be given the opportunity to lead a research group of her own, and McGill wasn't offering her a permanent position as a professor.

Harriet spent two years at Barnard, but when she announced that she was engaged, she was told that she was expected to resign. At that time, it was believed that being a wife would interfere with a woman's capacity to do her job. The head of the physics department pleaded to keep Harriet, but the policy was not changed. In the meantime, although Harriet had ended her engagement, she still resigned from Barnard. Upset by the unfairness of the situation, she was quoted as saying: "I think it is a duty I owe to my profession and to my sex to show that a woman

Marie Curie is one of the most renowned scientists in history. Not only did she discover radioactivity as a property in certain elements, but she also found that it could be used to treat tumors. She devoted her whole life to science and won the Nobel Prize in both chemistry and physics.

has a right to the practice of profession and cannot be condemned to abandon it merely because she marries."

Harriet found comfort with some new and interesting friends she made while in New York City. One was Maxim Gorky, a Russian writer exiled from his home because of his controversial belief that Russia should no longer be ruled by a monarch. Harriet traveled across Europe with Gorky and his friends, inspired by their ideas about equality for all people and enjoying discussions about how to create a better world.

Harriet with her husband and their children, Barbara, Charles and Paul, around 1921.

In this atmosphere of excitement, perhaps change seemed possible to Harriet. She decided to return to her scientific career. Moving to Paris, Harriet joined Marie Curie's famous research group and continued to study radioactivity.

Harriet returned to Montreal in 1907 to marry Frank Pitcher, an engineer she met while at McGill, and withdrew from the scientific world to raise her three children. Her research continued to influence other scientists, but her role was not always acknowledged. In 1909, Otto Hahn, a German scientist who had worked with Rutherford at McGill, recreated one of Harriet's experiments, published his results, and took all the credit for himself.

Over time, Harriet's name faded from what had become the established field of radioactivity. It is only recently that her significant contributions have been rediscovered. These days, Harriet Brooks Pitcher is mentioned in textbooks and is recognized as an outstanding scientist. And when you look at your periodic table in science class and see the element radon, you will know whose pioneering efforts put it there!

4

MARIA GOEPPERT-MAYER

1906–1972

As a girl, Maria Goeppert loved to entertain guests by playing Schubert tunes for them on the piano. Her parents were well known in the community of Göttingen, Germany, where her father was a respected professor of pediatrics at the university. Many of the guests at the Goeppert house were prominent scientists, and young Maria's energy and her lively piano playing charmed them. They assumed that she would become a wife and mother. What they didn't know was that Maria would also grow up to be one of the greatest scientists of the twentieth century.

Maria's father wanted his daughter to be educated, and encouraged her interest in science. He taught her what he knew about nature during walks in the thick woods surrounding Göttingen, and he once built her a pair of special glasses so she could observe a solar *eclipse*. Maria greatly admired her father, the sixth generation of Goepperts to be a university professor, and hoped to uphold that tradition. This was very ambitious for a young girl at that time — the talented mathematician Emily Noether had just been refused a position at the University of Göttingen only because she was a woman!

The special girls' school that Maria had attended to prepare her for the grueling entrance exams for university closed the year before she was ready to take the tests. She could not attend any of the other schools in town because they did not accept girls. With no school to go to, Maria and a few other girls decided to form a study group and take the university exams a year early. All the girls passed, and Maria entered the University of Göttingen in 1924.

Maria loved the atmosphere at the university. There was an air of excitement in the physics department as scientists learned about the intriguing and mysterious *atom*. Atoms are too small to see even under a microscope — and are made up of even smaller parts called *electrons*, *protons* and *neutrons* — but they make up everything in our world.

One of Maria's professors, Max Born, introduced her to the branch of physics called *quantum mechanics*, which explores what an atom looks like. In other words, how the smallest particles in atoms interact with one another: how they are organized, how they move, and what happens when they move. The more Maria studied the atom, the more questions she had about it. There was still so much that needed to be discovered!

After classes, Maria and her friends would often meet in town for dinner. Sitting around the table, they would each offer their own solution to the problems presented in their classes. The plates in front of them would be forgotten as they spent hours having heated debates about their theories.

Her father's death in 1927 was a great loss for Maria, since he was the one who had first triggered her love for science. To support the family, Maria's mother took in boarding students. One of the first to arrive at the Goeppert household was Joseph Mayer, a young American from California. He came to Göttingen to study quantum mechanics, the field in which Maria was quickly becoming an expert.

A model of the atom. Electrons orbit around the center, called the nucleus, which is made up of protons and neutrons. Maria came up with a new model for how the nucleus is constructed.

It didn't take long for Joseph and Maria to become good friends. Once, when Maria was having difficulty solving a complicated physics problem for her *thesis*, Joseph took her to visit the physicist Paul Ehrenfest. After listening to Maria for a few minutes, Paul offered her his guest room so she could sit down and finish the problem. Nearly the only decorations in the room were the autographs of famous scientists, including Albert Einstein, on the walls. Maria contemplated the signatures for a few minutes, then solved the problem within an hour. She scrawled her own name alongside the rest before she left the room.

In 1930, Maria received her *Ph.D.* in physics at the young age of twenty-four. She was now qualified to work as a university professor, just like her father.

Around the same time, Joseph and Maria got married. They decided to move to the United States so Joseph could take a teaching position at Johns Hopkins University in Baltimore, Maryland. Maria hoped that Johns Hopkins would offer her a position as well. She was disappointed to learn that they would not hire her because her husband had a job there. They did not want to be accused of favoritism. Maria tried not to be disheartened. In order to continue working on physics problems, she began what would become a trend in her scientific career — she became a volunteer.

Maria taught classes, supervised graduate students and did research at Johns Hopkins without ever being paid! When she asked if she could have an office, the university cleared out a small space in the attic for her.

Maria was experiencing the challenges of being a woman in the male-dominated world of science. Despite all the work she was doing for Johns Hopkins, the university refused even to print her name in the school's course catalogue as a research associate. And after her daughter and son were born, Maria experienced tremendous pressure to give up her research, since it was still not seen as acceptable for women to be working mothers. But she was not ready to abandon her dream of becoming one of the best physicists in the world.

In 1938, the Mayers moved to New Jersey so Joseph could take a job at Columbia University in New York City. Maria was made very unwelcome at the university. Once again she had to settle for being a volunteer. She was not even invited to attend university dinners because she was a woman. She and Joseph co-wrote a textbook for the university called *Statistical Mechanics*, but, as often happened to female co-authors, the administration listed her only as an editorial assistant.

Although she was treated unfairly, Maria tried not to let her frustration show. Her daughter Marianne once remarked that Maria felt "that she had to behave properly if she was not to be accused of being a conniving, abrasive woman." Maria did not want to encourage any of the stereotypes that surrounded women.

When World War II broke out in 1939, society was forced to put some of those stereotypes aside. There was a shortage of men to fill jobs and women began to be considered for jobs that had been closed to them. Maria accepted a teaching position at Sarah Lawrence College, a prestigious women's college. It was her first paying job as a scientist.

Maria teaching at Sarah Lawrence College in the 1940s

© Bettmann/CORBIS/MAGMA

Once the war ended, Maria and Joseph decided to move to Chicago. As usual, the university refused to pay her. But two things happened which created new opportunities for Maria. First, she was reunited with some of her friends from Göttingen. Lots of research about the atom had been done during the war and Maria could discuss these new findings with her friends. By splitting the tiny atom, scientists had created the *atomic bomb*. What else could be done with the atom, they wondered?

NUCLEAR ENERGY

An atom of a radioactive element has an incredible amount of energy in its nucleus, or core. This energy is very powerful and is used to produce electricity. It is also how the sun creates light and heat. To release this energy you must either use fusion, the joining of two atoms, or fission, the splitting of a single atom. A woman named Lise Meitner helped discover the fission method!

Then Maria was reunited with one of her former students, Bob Sachs, who was working outside of Chicago at the Argonne National Laboratory. He knew how brilliant his teacher was and offered Maria a research job at Argonne. There she began to learn about *nuclear physics*, which is the study of the core (*nucleus*) of the atom.

Despite its size, researchers were finding that a lot goes on inside an atom. Maria began investigating why some atoms produce *nuclear energy* and others do not. She realized that if the questions about the nucleus of the atom were ever to be solved, there needed to be a new model of the nucleus.

Maria took on the challenge of designing this new model. The idea that the nucleus is constructed like the layers of an onion, with protons and neutrons orbiting in the layers, had been suggested in an earlier model, but this model had not quite worked. Maria completed the model by adding the idea of *spin-orbit coupling*. Spin-orbit coupling shows that protons and neutrons have different amounts of energy depending on which way they spin within their orbit. Maria had just formulated the *nuclear shell model*. Now scientists could begin to understand why some atoms produced nuclear energy and others did not. Barely a week after Maria formulated her theory, some of her colleagues were already teaching it in their classes!

As she began to prepare to publish her findings, Maria learned that another scientist, Hans Jensen, had made the same discovery at about the same time. She and Jensen decided that instead of being competitors, they would be more effective as collaborators. The book they wrote together about the nuclear shell model was published in 1955. The model allowed scientists to better understand certain atoms and nuclear energy.

Despite her incredible discovery, it would take Maria ten years to receive the one thing that she had always wanted. In 1960, Maria was finally offered a full professorship at the University of San Diego. When the University of Chicago discovered they were going to lose Maria, they were suddenly prepared to offer her a paying position! It was too late. Maria and Joseph moved to California.

The Nobel Prize is an international award that has been given out yearly since 1901 for achievements in physics, chemistry, medicine, literature, economics and peace. The prize was founded by Alfred Nobel, who invented dynamite in 1866. Maria was only the second woman to win the prize in physics. But women were still not regarded as true scientists even in the 1960s. A San Diego newspaper ran the headline "S.D. Mother Wins Nobel Prize"!

As she got older, Maria found it more difficult to teach and do research. Then something happened that lifted her spirits. One day in 1963, the phone rang at four o'clock in the morning. Joseph sleepily answered it, and a man with a thick Swedish accent asked to interview Maria. Joe passed Maria the phone, and the journalist at the other end asked her how she felt about winning the Nobel Prize. Maria had won the Nobel Prize in physics! After years of struggling to be accepted as a professional scientist, she was being honored with the most prestigious scientific award in the world. She flew to Sweden to receive the award, which she shared with Jensen. A woman had not received the award in physics since Marie Curie in 1903, and no other woman has won the prize in that category since then.

Maria's passion for science helped her overcome the many barriers she faced throughout her career. After receiving the Nobel Prize, she remarked that "Winning the prize wasn't half as exciting as doing the work itself."

5

RACHEL CARSON

1907–1963

Imagine a world in which no one cared that rivers were dark and murky from pollution, that insects, birds and fish were dying, and that forests and shorelines were being destroyed. Without Rachel Carson, many of us would not know about the importance of protecting our environment.

Growing up in the small farming community of Springdale, Pennsylvania, Rachel was a lonely child. Her siblings were all older than her and there were few children to play with. But Rachel and her mother took long walks in the vast fields and wild forests surrounding Springdale, and Rachel quickly formed a deep kinship with the living world.

Once she started school, Rachel's interests grew to include reading and writing. Combining her loves, she read books set in the wild like *The Wind in the Willows* and *The Story of Peter Rabbit*. Inspired by these stories, Rachel wrote her own. She submitted some to a children's magazine and was pleased when the magazine published them. Encouraged by her success, Rachel decided to become a writer.

There was no high school in Springdale, so when Rachel finished elementary school she and a few other students gathered every day to be tutored. It became clear that Rachel had the talent to go to college, but her parents felt that she needed to attend a real high school first.

Rachel traveled several hours a day to get to and from the high school in a neighboring town. She was very shy and not used to being surrounded by so many people her age, so she generally kept to herself, always staying focused on her studies.

Rachel knew that she needed to earn a *scholarship* to go to college, since her parents had very little money. Having put her mind to it, Rachel graduated in 1925 at the top of her class. She was accepted to Pennsylvania College for Women — with the scholarship she needed!

Living away from home for the first time and feeling that she did not always fit in meant that college was another big adjustment. Rachel became more comfortable with college life once she became more confident in her classes. She joined some sports teams and had fun cooking big breakfasts with her roommate.

At first, Rachel took lots of English classes. She was not particularly interested in science and delayed taking the required science class for as long as she could. When she finally registered for a *biology* course, it changed her life.

Rachel was surprised by how much she enjoyed biology, and how it helped her to understand the natural world she loved to observe.

As Rachel's interest in biology grew, she spent more time in the laboratories and talking with her professor, an intelligent, elegant and independent woman named Mary Scott Skinker. Instead of giving in to pressure to marry and give up her career, Skinker had chosen to pursue a Ph.D. in *zoology*, the study of animal behavior. She showed Rachel that women could succeed in science, and encouraged her to continue her studies. When it came time for Rachel to choose the main subject of her college degree, she surprised everybody, including herself, by choosing science.

Rachel in the laboratory

Rachel used her passion for biology to do graduate studies in zoology at Johns Hopkins University in Baltimore, Maryland. Because Rachel continued to earn high grades, she was invited to spend her summer at Woods Hole, a marine biology laboratory on the coast of Massachusetts which was affiliated with Johns Hopkins. There, by the Atlantic Ocean, Rachel quickly became fascinated by the beauty and mysteries of the sea. She wanted to know more about the ocean and about how the animals that lived under those massive waves survived. She was discovering the world of *ecology*, the study of an environment and the different species that live within it.

While at Johns Hopkins, Rachel had other obligations

besides her studies. She had always felt a strong sense of responsibility, and since her parents had retired and her siblings were not in a position to help out financially, she found work teaching to support the family. She moved them to Baltimore and made the difficult decision to become a part-time student. Determined to finish her degree, she finally received her master's in the spring of 1932. It was a proud day after three years of hard work.

That fall, Rachel began her *Ph.D.*, the highest degree that a person can achieve at university. She struggled, however, with having to juggle work and school. Finally she left school to find full-time work.

Rachel went to the United States Bureau of Fisheries, where she knew a few people through her former teacher, Mary Scott Skinker. The Bureau wanted to produce a radio series to inform the public about its work, but it seemed that no one could make this work understandable and exciting. Rachel was asked to give it a try. Although she had not done much writing since her early college days, she needed the money and so she jumped at the chance. Her captivating and poetic writing so deeply impressed her superiors that the Bureau hired her full time. She edited reports and wrote brochures, and she traveled to different conservation areas to learn about the lives of the fish in the sea.

While reading a report about the decline of the fish population,

Rachel writing by the seaside

Rachel decided she could turn it into an article for the general public. She was still struggling financially, and this would be another way to earn some money. Rachel began writing articles about ecological issues for local newspapers.

In 1936, the Fisheries Bureau assigned Rachel to write an introduction for one of their brochures. Inspired by the ocean and all its wonders, she got carried away and produced an eleven-page essay. It was a bit long for an introduction, but her boss immediately suggested that Rachel try to sell it to the renowned magazine *Atlantic Monthly*. At first, Rachel scoffed at the idea. It was one thing to sell articles to local newspapers, but a completely different one to try to be published in a prestigious magazine sold nationwide! She put her insecurities aside, though, and sent her essay.

To her surprise and delight, the magazine published the piece. Readers loved the way the article introduced them to the mysterious world of the ocean. Rachel was shocked when an editor from Simon and Schuster Publishers approached her, asking her to extend the article into a full-length book. Unexpectedly, Rachel's dream of becoming a writer was coming true and she was writing about what she loved best — nature.

Under the Sea-Wind came out in November 1941. Due to the outbreak of World War II, however, the book received very little attention and did not sell very well. Rachel was disappointed. It seemed that her literary career, which had barely begun, had already stalled. She continued to work for the government, but moved to the Fish and Wildlife Service, where she learned more about the effects

Rachel's second book, *The Sea Around Us*, won the National Book Award, the Burroughs Medal for excellence in nature writing, and spent 31 weeks at number one on the *New York Times* bestseller list.

humans have on the environment of these creatures.

Rachel's heart was in writing, however, and she was not ready to give up because of one disappointment. Besides, she wanted the public to understand just how special and important nature is to the lives of humans. Her second book, *The Sea Around Us*, explained how the oceans were formed, and highlighted their vital role on earth. It was one of the first books to explain to the general public how humans, animals and nature are all interconnected.

The Sea Around Us became a bestseller and received the National Book Award. Critics were amazed at Rachel's talent for accurately describing nature in a way that was interesting and easy to understand. Rachel felt she could finally leave her job at the government and dedicate herself to writing full time.

Due to the controversy surrounding Rachel's last book, *Silent Spring*, the American television network CBS decided to air an hour-long special on pesticides that included an interview with Rachel. The show went on despite the withdrawal of three sponsors in protest. Rachel was filmed with both a government official and a chemist from a pesticide company that strongly opposed Rachel's book. Both admitted that they were unaware of the negative effects of pesticide use. The interview brought the issue to a wide audience and is considered an important piece of journalism.

She moved to the coast of Maine for her next project, a shore guide explaining the different species that live in and around the ocean. As Rachel did her research, what had started out as a shore guide evolved into a book about how all the species in the sea rely on each other for survival. *The Edge of the Sea* was published in 1955, and was another huge success. It helped solidify Rachel's reputation as an ecological expert.

Before she could decide what her next book would be about, tragedy struck her family. Rachel's niece

Marjorie died, and Rachel decided to adopt Marjorie's son. While she was coping with these difficulties, a new threat entered her life. Developers wanted to build on one of Rachel's favorite places, the woods near her Maine home. Rachel began to act to promote the importance of natural *conservation.*

Around the same time, Rachel received a letter from a woman who believed that *pesticides*, powerful chemicals used to kill insects on crops, were also harming the wildlife in her area. Rachel began to investigate. She gathered research showing that the pesticide *DDT* was causing cancer in animals and having other harmful effects on them. This suggested that if humans were eating foods that had been sprayed with DDT, it might be making them sick as well. As Rachel looked at more and more evidence, she knew what her next book needed to be about.

When it became known that Rachel's new project would expose how the environment was being attacked, she began one of her biggest struggles yet. Companies that produced pesticides criticized her and denied her access to research reports. She had to rely on some of her old friends at the Fish and Wildlife Service to sneak her results from studies they were doing.

When Rachel's final book, *Silent Spring*, went on sale, the news magazine *Time* wrote that the book was an "emotional and inaccurate outburst." Years later, however, the magazine gave her the credit she deserved. They named her one of the 20 most influential scientists of the 20th century! Rachel was one of only two women on the list.

Rachel was also fighting breast cancer. She was often ill and in the hospital, but was determined to get her book written. The world needed to know the danger that the environment was in. Rachel persisted, putting in many hours of research and writing.

Even before her book *Silent Spring* came out in 1962, controversy swirled around it. Some pesticide-producing companies tried to stop the book from being published, and Rachel was accused of being a hysterical woman who was exaggerating the effects of pesticides. But the book sold well, and when President John F. Kennedy read it, he decided to form a committee to study the effects of pesticides. The results showed that Rachel's findings were correct. This led to the establishment of the Environmental Protection Agency, which began to study and regulate the uses of chemicals on the environment.

On April 14, 1963, Rachel died of cancer. Her work, however, lives on. In 1969 DDT was banned in Canada, and in 1972 it was banned in the United States. Rachel is also credited with starting the environmental movement in North America.

Rachel Carson not only made people interested in nature, she made them care about it. And she started the fight to save it.

6

CHIEN-SHIUNG WU

1912–1997

If you hold a stone in the palm of your hand and let it drop, it always falls to the ground. That simple action is an example of the law of *gravity*, one of the *laws of nature*. These laws apply to every reaction and interaction in nature, and scientists rely on these laws to further their understanding of the world. Well, imagine that one day you picked up a stone and let it go, and instead of dropping, it shot upwards into the air. You would be shocked and confused about what you were seeing, and would have to re-examine the way you see and understand nature. Chien-Shiung Wu, a brilliant physicist, caused exactly this kind of stunned reaction in the scientific community when she overturned one of the basic laws of nature.

Chien-Shiung was born May 31, 1912 in the small village of Liuhe, a few miles outside of Shanghai in China. Her father gave his daughter a name that means "courageous hero," because he hoped that she would overcome the common belief at the time that women could not achieve as much as men. He refused to bind her feet, a painful and crippling tradition in parts of China. And he told her to "ignore the obstacles and keep walking ahead."

In parts of China, the feet of young girls were traditionally tightly wrapped so that they could not grow properly. Small feet were considered beautiful and also meant that women were not very mobile and therefore easier to control.

Chien-Shiung's father ran the first school that she attended, a small building where classes only went as far as grade four. To continue her education, she had to travel to the Suzhou Girls' School, a boarding school over fifty miles away. Chien-Shiung could only see her family on weekends and during summer holidays.

At the Suzhou Girls' School, Chien-Shiung enrolled in a teacher-training program because she would be guaranteed a job when she graduated. One day she overheard a conversation between some of her friends who were in an academic program, and realized that they were learning more science than she was. Chien-Shiung decided to borrow their textbooks and stay up late into the night so that she could teach herself. As she studied chemistry, physics and mathematics, she found that the physics problems were her favorites.

Chien-Shiung graduated in 1930 at the top of her class. She didn't even have to apply to university — she was hand-picked to go to the elite National Central University in

Nanjing. Chien-Shiung wanted to study physics at university but worried that she wasn't well enough prepared. Her father surprised her with some science books when she went home for the summer. He was proud of Chien-Shiung and wanted to help her in any way he could. The books allowed her to study over the summer and renewed her confidence.

There was a great deal of turmoil in China at the time, since Japan was threatening to invade and take over the country. Chien-Shiung had a deep love for China and she was opposed to anyone taking away its independence. In university she organized student protests and a boycott of Japanese products. For one demonstration, she led students into the courtyard of the Chinese President's home. After several hours, the President finally came out to hear what the students had to say. They urged him to stand firm against Japan and he agreed to do what he could. For the rest of her life, Chien-Shiung was never afraid to voice her opinion, whether it was political or scientific.

Chien-Shiung graduated from university in 1934. Two years later she made the difficult decision to leave her family and her beloved China to pursue a graduate degree in physics. None of the schools in China offered the program, so she planned to earn her degree as quickly as possible and then return to China to help improve the country. But as Chien-Shiung boarded the boat to sail to the United States, she didn't know that she was seeing her family for the last time.

When Chien-Shiung arrived in the

The Wu Chien-Shiung Educational Foundation (in China they say a person's family name before their given name) runs a science camp in Taipei, Taiwan for high school and college students from around the world. The students have the chance to meet scientists and learn more about their favorite areas of science.

United States she registered at Berkeley University in San Francisco, California. It took her some time to adjust to American ways. She didn't really like the cafeteria food and was happy to find some local Chinese restaurants. She also chose to continue wearing her clothes from China, which looked very different from those worn by most North American women. Chien-Shiung was proud of her heritage, and didn't feel the need to hide it.

After barely a year at Berkeley, Chien-Shiung was devastated to learn that Japan had invaded China after all. All communication with China was cut off, so she could not find out what had happened to her family. To make matters worse, she kept seeing newspaper articles about how badly the Japanese were treating the people of China. The only way she could cope was to throw herself into her work. She often stayed in the laboratory until three a.m., working on her experiments.

In 1990, an asteroid — which is like a very small planet revolving around the sun, usually between the orbits of Mars and Jupiter — was named for Chien-Shiung. She was the first living scientist to have an asteroid bear her name!

In 1940 Chien-Shiung received her *Ph.D.* in physics. She stayed at Berkeley for two more years as a research assistant. By then the United States had entered World War II, and because they were fighting against Japan, a great deal of discrimination against Asian people was occurring. Berkeley refused to offer Chien-Shiung a full-time position, but she tried not to be discouraged. She had just married Luke Yuan, a Chinese-born physicist she had met at Berkeley, and the couple decided to move to New York. Chien-Shiung got a teaching job at Smith College, but she missed the challenges of research.

Because of World War II, there came to be a shortage of

physicists in the United States. Many of the universities that had refused to hire Chien-Shiung because of her gender and race were now seeking her out. She agreed to teach at Princeton University in New Jersey. Chien-Shiung was the first female professor at Princeton — the university wasn't even admitting female students yet!

After a short while at Princeton, Chien-Shiung was asked to move to New York City to join a team of researchers at Columbia University. They were working on the American military's top-secret Manhattan Project, trying to build an *atomic bomb* before the Nazis did. Many of the best scientists in the world took part, but Chien-Shiung was one of only a few who were asked to stay on at Columbia after the war had ended to teach and do research.

THE MANHATTAN PROJECT
In June 1942, World War II was raging. The Nazis had gained territory in Europe and were rumored to be building an atomic bomb, a very destructive weapon that many thought would decide who won the war. The United States felt that in order to protect themselves and the countries they were allied with, they would need to build one first. 140,000 people worked on the project. The American laboratories finished an atomic bomb first.

After the war, Chien-Shiung finally discovered that her family was safe. She missed them very much, and after giving birth to her son in 1947, she began to consider moving back to China. Once again, though, world events stood in her way. A Communist political group had taken over China, and Chien-Shiung and her husband were advised to stay in North America. They decided that it was time to apply for American citizenship, which was granted to them in 1954.

To deal with homesickness for her family and for China, Chien-Shiung dedicated most of her time to research. She was known for working seven days a week. During this time

Atoms are the tiniest units of an element that still have the features of that element. Elements are the basic substances that make up all matter. For example, the elements oxygen and hydrogen make up water. Atoms have a central nucleus — consisting of smaller particles called protons and neutrons — that is surrounded by a third kind of particle called an electron.

she became particularly interested in a phenomenon called *beta decay*, a process that occurs in the *nucleus* or the center of an atom. The famous physicist Enrico Fermi had come up with a theory about beta decay, which many other scientists had tried unsuccessfully to prove. Chien-Shiung designed her own experiment and became the first to demonstrate that Fermi had been correct. This achievement solidified her reputation as one of the best physicists in the world.

Other physicists began to consult Chien-Shiung when they had a problem they couldn't solve. In 1956, two researchers, Tsung Dao Lee and Chen Ning Yang, approached her with a theory that they had not yet found a way to prove.

For thirty years, scientists had believed in the principle of *conservation of parity*. The word "parity" itself generally means that things are equal. In physics, parity refers to a symmetry in nature that scientists always expected their research to confirm. For example, imagine that two experiments are set up in such a way that they are mirror images of one another. According to the law of conservation of parity, just as if you looked in a mirror and raised your left arm while your mirror image raised its right, scientists expected that if in one of these two experiments movement occurred to the left, in the other it would occur to the right. Scientists thought that the law of conservation of parity was as reliable as the law of gravity, and would often tailor their results to fit the theory.

But Lee and Yang's research was beginning to suggest

that parity conservation did not always occur. They needed Chien-Shiung's remarkable talent for building and running experiments to find out if they were correct. Chien-Shiung was not convinced by their theory, but she devised an elaborate and ambitious experiment. She joined forces with the National Bureau of Standards in Washington, D.C. because their laboratory had the equipment needed. For months she traveled between New York and Washington to work on the experiment, her enthusiasm keeping her going whenever she got tired.

The hard work of Chien-Shiung and her partners in the experiment paid off — the results astonished the scientific world. The law of conservation of parity did not always exist inside the nucleus of an atom! This was as surprising to scientists as it would be to you if your mirror image acted differently than you had expected. Physicists had to rethink many of their former assumptions, and Chien-Shiung's findings also opened many new possibilities for research

Chien-Shiung at work in her laboratory at Columbia University, in New York City, where she taught and researched for thirty-seven years!

into the great mysteries of the universe. Lee and Yang were awarded the Nobel Prize in Physics in 1957, and many people feel that Chien-Shiung was unfairly left out.

But Chien-Shiung did not let this bother her. She herself went on to win the National Medal of Science, the top American award for scientific achievement. She was also elected to the National Academy of Sciences, becoming the first woman to win the Academy's Comstock Award along the way. Her research career was so impressive that she became the first woman to be president of the American Physical Society and to receive an honorary doctorate in science from Princeton. Chien-Shiung remained at Columbia for the rest of her career, and began to give lectures encouraging young women to study science.

She also finally got to return to China. Her family had passed away by then, but Chien-Shiung still wanted to accomplish one of the goals she had set out to do — to modernize the sciences in her homeland. She visited several times to give lectures, and even granted a student award in her name. She retired in 1981 after a brilliant career. As the *New York Post* put it, "This small modest woman was powerful enough to do what armies can never accomplish; she helped destroy a law of nature."

7

ROSALIND FRANKLIN

1920–1958

The discovery of deoxyribonucleic acid, or *DNA* as we know it, changed the way we understand the human body. DNA acts like a blueprint in our bodies that carries our *genes*. Genes hold the codes to the traits that we inherit from our parents and grandparents. Our genes determine the color of our eyes and how tall we grow. Understanding DNA has helped scientists figure out whether individuals are likely to be born with certain illnesses or disabilities. It has also helped them learn how to prevent or cure these problems. DNA also provides a genetic "fingerprint" that can help scientists identify who committed a given crime. And our understanding of DNA has turned ideas like cloning, which once seemed like a fairy tale, into reality.

We know as much as we do about DNA because of the work of a remarkable scientist, Rosalind Franklin. Her important role in uncovering the shape of DNA was almost forgotten because she was a woman in the male world of science.

London, England in the 1920s was a prosperous and lively place. World War I had just ended and people were beginning to enjoy life again after many years of suffering. Women especially were seeing their lives changing. During the war, they had performed many jobs usually reserved for men, including factory work, and had gone to the battle-fields to nurse wounded soldiers. Women worked hard and enjoyed the sense of freedom that employment gave them. So when men came back from fighting and women were told to go back to their old lives, many refused. They wanted to continue working, and began to protest and seek the same rights and privileges as men. Changes were being made and women did gain certain rights, like being able to vote, but old ways of thinking persisted.

Rosalind Franklin was born on July 25, 1920, just as all this change was going on. Throughout her life she would find herself in the middle of the struggle between old and new ways of perceiving women.

Most of the people in Rosalind's family were very open-minded, and some of her relatives were involved in the protests for women's rights. Growing up, Rosalind was never made to feel inferior to boys. She played rough games with her three brothers and competed fiercely against them. She was also independent and strong willed. On one occasion she got a needle stuck in her knee, and, not wanting to appear weak (a typical stereotype about women), she walked all the way to the hospital with that needle still sticking out!

In her teens, Rosalind went to St. Paul Girls' School in London. She was a good student and was always very hardworking. While she was there, she discovered that she loved science; its logic appealed to her practical nature. She was also an adventurer at heart, and there was no greater landscape to explore than the mysterious world of science.

When Rosalind finished high school and wanted to go to university, her father refused to help her. He told Rosalind that higher education was useless to women and that she would have to be satisfied with doing volunteer work. Although disappointed by her father's reaction, Rosalind was not deterred. One of her aunts offered to help pay her tuition and her mother also supported her. It was not long before her father changed his mind and soon Rosalind was off to Newnham College, at Cambridge University, one of the oldest and most famous schools in England.

By 1941, Rosalind had earned a *bachelor's degree* in science and had begun doing graduate studies. University is often a fun and happy time when young people get to make new friends and learn new ideas. But women were still excluded from many activities at Cambridge, and life there was not always pleasant.

Fortunately, Rosalind found a friend in Adrienne Weill, a scientist from France who understood the frustrations of being a woman in the world of science. Weill taught Rosalind French and encouraged her to believe that change was possible.

This was in the middle of World

The Rosalind Franklin Award was established in 2002 to honor Rosalind's scientific achievements. The award is given for an outstanding contribution in natural science, engineering or technology.

59

War II, and Rosalind wanted to make a contribution to the war effort. She took a job with the British Coal Utilization Research Association, where she was given a lot of independence. Rosalind soon discovered that she worked best under those conditions.

It was a frightening time in England. German planes would fly over the country dropping bombs. Rosalind had to ride her bicycle to work through fields that were targeted, swerving and ducking to protect herself. Her hard work and courage paid off, and she was awarded a doctorate degree for her research on carbons, the main substance in coal.

Once the war ended, Rosalind accepted a position in Paris, a city that seemed more exciting and modern than London. Her cramped room was a huge change from the big house and servants she was used to in London, but Rosalind loved Paris. She felt that women there were treated equally and with respect. The men that she worked with regarded her first and foremost as a scientist, and there was a team spirit at the laboratory that she had never before experienced.

It was in Paris that Rosalind learned the important technique of *x-ray crystallography*, a method used to try to

Facts About DNA

There are one hundred trillion (100,000,000,000,000) cells in your body, each of which contain DNA.

Humans have approximately 30,000 genes.

If all the strands of DNA in your body were laid out end to end, they would reach to the sun and back over 600 times.

Human DNA is 98% identical to that of a chimpanzee!

identify the materials and structure of matter that is too small to be seen with the eye or a microscope.

In 1951, John Randall, the head of the laboratory at King's College back in England, offered Rosalind a challenge that she could not refuse. He asked her to work on mapping the structure of DNA.

Johann Friedrich Miescher first discovered DNA, which is found in the cells of all living things, in 1869. By the late 1940s scientists understood that DNA controls heredity, but they still didn't know how it actually works. How does DNA pass genes — units of hereditary codes — from parents to their children? The key was in finding the structure of DNA. A race was on to do exactly this and Rosalind was about to become one of the contestants.

Rosalind arrived at King's College expecting to set up an x-ray crystallography lab and work on the DNA problem with the help of a student. Maurice Wilkins, another scientist working at King's, thought that Rosalind was hired to be his assistant. This created a very tense atmosphere and they decided to work independently from each other.

Of all the researchers — James Watson, Francis Crick, Maurice Wilkins and Rosalind Franklin — only Rosalind had a university degree in chemistry.

In the meantime, James Watson and Francis Crick were also working on the DNA mystery. Instead of taking x-rays, they were trying to build an actual model of a strand of DNA. When one of their attempts failed, their supervisor at Cambridge University told them to give up. But the prospect of receiving credit for such a significant discovery was too tempting, and they continued their work in secret.

Rosalind made quick progress at King's College. She discovered that DNA existed in two forms, A and B, and took x-rays of both so she could analyze the images. DNA is made up of different pieces, and a crucial part of mapping its structure is making sure that each piece is in the right place. It was painstaking work, but Rosalind was meticulous, precise and patient. She toiled away with the help of a student, Raymond Gosling. Sometimes they used food fights as a way to release some of their frustration!

But Rosalind felt very isolated. Bad feelings between her and Wilkins and the old-fashioned policies at King's College — for example, women were barred from the Commons Room — made it clear that Rosalind and other women were unwelcome at the school.

Despite these difficult circumstances, Rosalind continued to make incredible progress. In 1952, she gave a lecture explaining some of her results to her audience. Sitting in the audience was James Watson, one of the other DNA researchers. If Watson had listened, he would have realized that Rosalind was sharing vital information about where some of the parts that make up DNA fit. Instead, he paid more attention to Rosalind's appearance, and later remarked that she would look prettier if she did something with her hair! Watson was unfortunately confirming Rosalind's belief that because she was a woman she was not always taken seriously as a scientist.

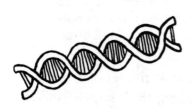

A diagram of a strand of DNA, showing the double helix shape that Rosalind discovered through her experiments.

Rosalind was close to making some conclusions at this point, but she was always cautious and wanted to be sure. In the meantime, the American scientist Linus Pauling was publishing his own theory about DNA. The race was heating up!

One day, in a meeting with

Watson, Maurice Wilkins complained about Rosalind's hesitation to publish her findings. Wilkins showed her research to Watson without her permission. Suddenly Watson and Crick had what they needed; the final clues to piece together their model.

In March of 1953, Rosalind prepared a paper stating her final conclusion — that DNA, the key to human genetics and heredity, is in the shape of a *double helix*. A double helix looks a bit like a twisted rope ladder. But Crick and Watson beat her to publication. Everybody acknowledged that this was an outstanding discovery. Since the use of her research was not even mentioned, no one, including Rosalind, recognized her pivotal role in this historic moment.

James Watson wrote a book about the discovery of the shape of DNA called *The Double Helix*. In it he gave a very unfair and unflattering portrayal of Rosalind. But in a later edition of the book, he added a new epilogue in which he acknowledged Rosalind's scientific talent. He admitted that the intensity of the competition to discover the shape of DNA had clouded his judgement of her.

With the structure of DNA revealed, Rosalind decided it was time to leave King's College. She still wanted to work on DNA, but she was not allowed to take her research with her. At Birkbeck College in London, she headed a team of scientists studying viruses. Rosalind published seventeen papers on her findings between 1953 and 1958. She also lectured on her work throughout Europe and North America.

Tragically, Rosalind died of cancer on April 16, 1958, before she had received proper recognition for her contribution to the DNA discovery. Four years later, Watson, Crick and Wilkins were awarded the Nobel Prize for their work on DNA. It will never be known whether Rosalind would have been included, since only living scientists can receive the award. As time has gone by, though, Rosalind's story has slowly emerged. That story exposes the discrimination that women in science have had to face, and gives Rosalind Franklin the credit she deserves for the discovery of the structure of DNA.

8

BIRUTÉ GALDIKAS

☆ ☆ ☆ ☆ ☆ ☆ ☆

1946–

On Christmas morning of 1971, Biruté Galdikas got exactly the present she wanted: she got to watch an orangutan emerging from her nest with her infant clutching her back. Not your typical Christmas present, but then again, celebrating Christmas in the jungles of Borneo is not your typical Christmas!

Biruté had been living in the dense rainforests of Indonesia to study orangutans for almost two months when this very special sighting occurred. Everyone had told her that studying orangutans would be impossible. Orangutans were too solitary, and roamed too much to be followed. But when Biruté saw that mother coming out of her nest, she knew there was hope for her study. She had seen this animal, which she named Beth, the day before, and finding her on this second day meant that Biruté had successfully tracked an orangutan!

By the age of six, Biruté had decided that she wanted to be an explorer. Growing up in Toronto, Canada, she began her adventures by riding the streetcars into the downtown area and exploring High Park, where she would hide near the willow trees to observe the ducks and turtles in the stream.

She also developed a fascination with ancient civilizations like the Incas and the Aztecs. Learning about these people who existed thousands of years ago led Biruté to wonder where exactly humans had come from. In high school, she studied orangutans. Looking at their hands and expressive brown eyes, she felt that somehow they must be connected to our own ancestors.

When Biruté was eighteen years old, she went to study at UCLA, a well-known university in Los Angeles, California. In one of her classes she heard about a woman who was studying chimpanzees in Africa. Suddenly, Biruté had a vision of her future. She must go to the rainforest and study orangutans. She had continued to read about them and had seen photographs in *National Geographic* and *Life* magazines. She realized very little was known about these beautiful red apes whose name means "people of the forest" in the Malay language. Many studies had been done in zoos,

There are four types of great apes — chimpanzees, gorillas, orangutans and bonobos. Apes differ from monkeys in several ways. They are more intelligent, and can even learn sign language. One gorilla named Koko was able to use up to 1,000 signs! Apes are also larger than monkeys, do not have tails, have fewer young and spend more time raising them. They spend more time upright and use their eyes more than their noses.

but very few had actually taken place in the natural habitat of orangutans — the rainforests of Indonesia and Malaysia. One of the longest studies had lasted eleven months. In that time the researcher had had such a hard time spotting orangutans that he had only managed to do ninety-two hours of direct observation, less than four days!

Jane Goodall was given a stuffed chimpanzee toy as a child, and it sparked a life-long interest in the animals. In 1965 she established a research camp to study them in Gombe National Park in Tanzania, Africa. Jane's observations showed that chimpanzees were highly intelligent. The research site is still in use, though Jane herself is usually traveling the world giving lectures about these animals.

This did not deter Biruté. She wrote to people who had studied orangutans and to the government of Malaysia, asking if they would be interested in supporting a study. No one replied. Biruté knew, though, that this was what she was meant to do and she was convinced that she could do it. She decided that if she could not find any support, then once she finished university, she would set off on her own, regardless of what anyone thought.

Biruté eventually learned that the woman studying chimpanzees in Africa was Jane Goodall, and the man who had helped her was the renowned *anthropologist* Louis Leakey. Anthropologists study human beings and their cultures. Leakey was particularly interested in the *evolution* of humans. With his partner and wife, Mary, he did excavations in Africa. They had unearthed bones from a skeleton that appeared to be an ancestor of ours who had lived about two million years ago!

Leakey was also very interested in studying the great apes — chimpanzees, gorillas, and orangutans — because of all the animals on the planet they are the most intelligent and most similar to humans. Leakey believed that the great

Dian Fossey visited Africa in 1963 and was fascinated by the gorillas she saw. She returned three years later for good, setting up the Karisoke Research Station high in the Virunga Mountains of Rwanda, Africa, where many gorillas lived. Her famous book, *Gorillas in the Mist*, was turned into a movie and brought knowledge of the creatures to a much wider audience. Dian began a campaign against the poachers who were killing gorillas, and it is thought that her murder in 1985 was related to this battle.

apes could provide insight into how our prehistoric ancestors had lived. With support from the National Geographic Society, he helped set up research camps for Jane Goodall to observe chimpanzees in Tanzania, Africa, and for Dian Fossey to observe mountain gorillas in Rwanda, Africa. He wanted to begin a study of orangutans but had heard how difficult this would be. Orangutans were known to be solitary creatures who lived well-hidden lives within the thick forests that are their homes.

Biruté had completed her undergraduate degree in 1966 and was working on her master's degree in *anthropology* when Leakey came to speak in one of her classes. This was her chance! Immediately after the lecture, she rushed up to Leakey, telling him that she was the right candidate for an orangutan study. Impressed by Biruté's determination, Leakey agreed to help her.

It took over two years to raise enough funds. In the meantime, Biruté completed her master's degree and waited patiently until she got word that she could go. Finally, in September 1971, when she was only twenty-five years old, Biruté left for Indonesia to begin her research.

Traveling with her husband, Biruté first went to Africa where she got to meet one of her heroes, Jane Goodall. Goodall gave her a tour of the camp she had set up and tips on how to study apes. Biruté was more excited than ever about exploring the world of orangutans.

It was a long trip to the study site. Biruté flew to the island of Borneo, took a speedboat up the Kumai River in the province of Kalimantan, then transferred into a dugout canoe. She and the people with her paddled up the murky waters into Tanjung Puting Park, a nature reserve, and finally to the small, dilapidated hut that would be her home. She named the grounds Camp Leakey and began to prepare for her study. But first she had to find the orangutans!

Biruté spent most of her days in the forest craning her neck, trying to spot an orangutan in the canopy of the tall rainforest. She usually returned to camp damp from the rain and with a sore neck. There were mosquitoes, flies, spiders and snakes, and with the rainy season came leeches. Despite the bites and sores, she tried not to be discouraged. She often heard the echoing calls of the orang-utans, and occasionally caught a glimpse of them swinging from tree to tree. This was already more than most people had thought she could achieve.

Then on that fateful Christmas day in 1971, Biruté started her second full day of observation of an orangutan. Her study had truly begun! She continued to watch Beth and her baby Bert over several days, making lots of notes about what they did. Although Beth didn't approach Biruté, she didn't run away from her either. Beth was becoming *habituated* — she was growing accustomed to the presence of a human.

Over time, Biruté followed many orangutans.

Biruté with young orangutans

Biruté in Borneo in 1991 with her son Frederick, then nine, and a large male orangutan.

Sometimes they would throw dead branches at her, trying to scare her away. Eventually, though, most came to accept her being there. Once one curious and energetic adolescent even scurried down the trunk of a tree until she was face to face with Biruté and could carefully inspect her. Biruté named all the orangutans to make it easier to keep track of them. She saw family sagas unfold as babies were born, grew from clingy children to rambunctious teenagers, and finally became independent adults.

Biruté even got her own opportunity to be an orangutan mother. Many people keep orangutans as pets even though it is illegal because orangutans are an endangered species. Biruté encouraged officials in Indonesia to confiscate illegally taken orangutans, but they often didn't. Sometimes Biruté herself managed to convince the owners to give up their pets so she could take them back to the jungle where they were meant to live. This was how little Sugito arrived at Camp Leakey. When he got there, he immediately adopted Biruté as his mother. This little ball of red fluff would follow her everywhere and would scream when he became separated from her. Sugito clung to Biruté all the time. She had to carry him with her into the forest when she went to make her *observations*. Biruté became mother to many orphaned orangutans as she continued to receive them at the camp.

By 1975, Biruté had gathered a great deal of information. In the 6800 hours she had spent observing orangutans, she had learned that they are semi-solitary rather than completely solitary. She had also observed that females give birth only once every eight or nine years, and that they spend most of their time searching for food and building their nests high in the trees to sleep at night. With the information, Biruté wrote her *dissertation* on this research, and received her *Ph.D.* degree in 1978. She had become the leading authority in the world on orangutans and their behavior.

Although Biruté's intention when she went to Indonesia was to study orangutans, she quickly realized that they were becoming endangered because their home was being destroyed. Loggers were cutting down many of the trees in Tanjung Puting Park and the orangutans had less and less space to search for food and to live. Biruté knew that in order to save the orangutans, she also had to save these beautiful forests.

One official told Biruté that the loggers would stop cutting down trees near the study area for as long as she was camped there. So she decided to stay, even if it meant forever. She once wrote, "To ever leave Tanjung Puting would be to betray it."

Fortunately, *National Geographic* magazine published a story Biruté had written about her experiences with

Male orangutans can weigh up to 220 pounds and can grow to a height of five feet, making them almost twice the size of females.

Orangutans can make simple tools, so that they can scratch themselves or poke into narrow spaces for food.

The orangutans Biruté has studied feed on over 400 different kinds of food — fruits, bark, flowers, insects, and sometimes bird eggs.

Today there are 15-25,000 orangutans in the world.

orangutans. People became interested in her work and she began to receive more support. She was able to build a proper rehabilitation center for orangutans that had been rescued from captivity, and in 1986 she started the Orangutan Foundation International, which promotes the preservation of orangutans around the world.

Biruté has made a huge difference through her work. The government of Taiwan has banned the import of apes into the country as pets. Certain countries have now agreed to make it illegal to sell a type of wood from the forests of Borneo, so loggers have stopped cutting down the trees. Tanjung Puting Park has now been expanded.

Almost everything we know about orangutans comes from Biruté's ongoing study. She now spends half the year in Vancouver, Canada, teaching anthropology at Simon Fraser University. The other half is spent in the rainforests of Borneo. Even after more than thirty years, Biruté loves this setting. She has said, "No matter which way I look, I always discover something new. Sometimes it is just the way a drop of water glistens on the end of a wet leaf or the way a spider's web becomes bejeweled with dew. Sometimes it is the sight of an insect that incongruously camouflages itself as a snowflake." And then of course there are the orangutans. Biruté still sees some of the same ones she encountered when she first arrived in 1971, and is still following the lives and behavior of these magnificent creatures she was told she would never even find.

9

CATHERINE HICKSON

1955–

May 18, 1980 began as a typical Sunday morning for the people living in the lush valleys surrounding Mount St. Helens. Suddenly, around 8:30, the ground shook and a huge explosion burst the calm. The blue sky vanished, engulfed by enormous clouds of gray ash. Mount St. Helens had erupted! For miles day turned to night, and everyone hurried to close their windows before the heavy ash could get in. The birds fell silent, their chirping replaced by a slithering sound like thousands of snakes coming down the streets, as over four inches of ash swept over everything in sight.

Closer to the mountain, the ferocity of the *volcano* was even more intense. The beautiful snowy peak of the mountain completely disappeared, blown away by the force of the eruption. One of the largest recorded landslides in history rocketed down the side of the mountain at speeds of up to 240 kilometers (150 miles) per hour. Walls of boiling mud fifteen meters (fifty feet) high gushed down from the top, incinerating everything in their path.

Catherine Hickson, a *geology* student, was camping only fourteen kilometers (almost nine miles) east of Mount St. Helens. The eruption changed her life. "Mount St. Helens was a show stopper! I had studied volcanoes, but to see this eruption up close and very personal was a career-changing event! If I hadn't already been in geology then I would have switched! During the event I was both scared to death and incredibly fascinated. I was hooked!"

Catherine is now a *volcanologist*, a person who studies volcanoes.

Being at Mount St. Helens was not Catherine's first experience with volcanoes. When she was five years old, she and her parents went to Yellowstone Park in the United States, a spectacular volcanic region. "I remember being totally overawed by the power of the *geysers* and the incredible beauty of the hot springs," she says. Geysers are considered volcanic because they erupt through the earth's surface. They are created when water that flows underground comes into contact with *magma*, rock that is so hot it is liquid. This causes the water to boil so violently that it

The word "volcano" actually comes from a volcanic island in the Mediterranean Sea. Long ago, people in the area saw smoke rising from the island and believed that it was the fireplace where the blacksmith Vulcan (a mythological figure) forged weapons for the Roman gods. They named the island Vulcano after him.

comes gushing out in a tall column of steam or water. Young Catherine, although she didn't know exactly why geysers explode the way they do, was spellbound by what she saw. She picked up her first piece of volcanic rock on that trip, and she still has it today.

> Polynesia is an area composed of the many islands in the southern part of the Pacific Ocean. The people living in this area have witnessed many impressive and destructive volcanic eruptions over the years. The local people used to believe that the eruptions occurred because they had somehow angered the goddess Pele.

Growing up in Edmonton, Alberta, Canada, Catherine developed many interests. Her summers were often spent at a cottage and traveling around Canada and the United States. On these trips she visited some of the most amazing natural sites in both countries, including the Rocky mountains and the Grand Canyon. Catherine loved being outdoors and enjoyed activities like canoeing, swimming and fishing, as well as collecting rocks, insects and leaves. She also adored animals and had many pets, including dogs, sheep and a horse.

At one time, Catherine considered becoming a veterinarian. But in the end, she decided to follow her love of sports and went to the University of Alberta, taking a recreation and physical education program. While in university, Catherine got married. She and her husband moved to California, and her studies were put on hold. When she returned to Alberta in 1977, she went back to school, this time in psychology. As a psychology student, she took several science courses. Her studies once again got interrupted when she moved to British Columbia.

Catherine registered at the University of British Columbia and continued in psychology. She had one more science elective to take, so she chose geology. In that course, she discovered that the natural history of the earth is actually tucked away in rocks. She also learned how the sites she had visited as a child were formed. These mysteries of the earth captivated her. "I quickly realized that this was where my heart was," she says about the impact the course had on her.

Although she had never really viewed being a geologist as a career for a woman, Catherine had found a field she truly loved and knew that it was the path that she wanted to follow. She switched into a geology program.

It was as a third year student that Catherine witnessed the eruption of Mount St. Helens. She had planned to focus on sedimentology, which explores a type of rock called sedimentary, but after her experience at Mount St. Helens, she knew that she needed to know more about volcanoes.

Volcanoes are formed when magma rises to the surface of the earth through rifts. Magma can reach temperatures of 12,000°F. As it is propelled through the crust of the earth it causes an eruption. These eruptions are usually accompanied by lava flows, *pyroclastic flows* (avalanches of hot rocks), and clouds of ash and gases, all of which leave

Catherine exploring an impact crater left from the eruption of Mount Lascar, Chile.

Volcano Facts

The country with the most volcanoes is Indonesia.

In the last 10,000 years, 1510 volcanoes have erupted.

The largest volcano in the world is Mauna Loa, in Hawaii.

The largest volcano in the solar system is Olympus Mons, on Mars.

The first volcanoes formed 3.5 billion years ago.

behind the mountainous shape of the volcano. Once a volcano is formed, it can erupt again as more magma escapes from the top. These eruptions can be very destructive. At Mount St. Helens, thousands of acres of forest were destroyed, millions of animals and insects perished, and sixty people died. Over time, though, volcanic eruptions provide benefits such as rich minerals for soil. Volcanologists study all these different aspects of volcanoes.

Catherine decided that she would be a volcanologist. Her studies included *fieldwork*, which meant visiting a volcanic site and studying it. On her first outing, Catherine bombarded her professor with questions. "I must have driven him mad," she recalls.

After receiving her *bachelor's degree* in 1982, Catherine immediately began a *master's degree*, then switched into the *Ph.D.* program.

During her studies, Catherine was surprised to discover that volcanoes existed in Canada, not far from where she lived. Wells Gray Park in southeastern British Columbia is filled with volcanoes, many of which have erupted within the past 10,000 years — which is not long ago in *geologic time*. Catherine made these volcanoes the focus of her work for her Ph.D. She did much of her research in Wells Gray Park,

Catherine leading an international field trip to examine some volcanoes.

her backpack filled with supplies such as maps, a geological hammer, a compass and an altimeter to measure the altitude. She spent many days, sometimes weeks, on mountainsides, patiently collecting samples of volcanic rock, analyzing them and mapping the area she was in. Catherine loved being out in the field, even after having encountered a grizzly bear! She was working outdoors, and at the same time discovering more and more incredible details about volcanoes.

Catherine's work at Wells Gray Park introduced her to a very particular kind of volcano: subglacial volcanoes, or volcanoes under ice. Around 10,000 years ago, British Columbia was covered in ice. Beneath the ice, volcanoes were erupting! Today these volcanoes are exposed but we can recognize that they were once submerged under glaciers by their frequently flat-topped shape. Subglacial volcanoes became one of Catherine's areas of specialty. She has studied them in both Canada and Iceland, where they are still erupting under ice.

Catherine received her Ph.D. in 1987, and since then she has continued her work on the volcanoes of British Columbia. She has made maps of their locations, and by looking at the products of these volcanoes, like lava and pyroclastic flows, she has created a better understanding of how these volcanoes erupt and whether they will one day erupt again.

Recently, Catherine has also been involved in an important project in the Andes mountains to learn more about the geology of this magnificent volcanic range, which stretches through Bolivia, Chile, Argentina and Peru. She has shared her expertise with volcanologists and geologists from the region and has helped them conduct their studies.

Catherine is now a professor at the University of British Columbia. She is also the head of the Vancouver office of the Geological Survey of Canada, whose main project is to gain a better understanding of the volcanoes in the Cordillera region of British Columbia, just west of the Rockies.

In 79 A.D. Mount Vesuvius erupted, causing lava flows to gush through the ancient Roman city of Pompeii in what is now Italy. Many citizens were killed because, while they had noticed rumblings a few days before, they had never imagined such destruction would occur and were caught unprepared. The event is famous in part because of the writings of an observer, a man named Pliny the Younger. He described in detail the earthquakes that shook the area before the eruption, the flows of lava and hot rocks, and the response of the people around him.

Catherine is also very involved in emergency preparedness, helping communities and research groups to be ready in case a volcano erupts. Mount Baker, a volcano in Washington State, is expected to erupt within the next century. Catherine has visited the area near Mount Baker to explain what people who live there should do if there is an eruption and what kind of damage could be caused by the volcano.

Catherine wants to carry on studying the volcanoes of Canada and hopes to make people more aware of them. Being able to combine her love of nature with her career is very rewarding, and her fascination with these mighty wonders just keeps growing. "Volcanoes are the epitome of the earth's power," she explains. "They show an incredible range of behavior. Finding out why different volcanoes erupt in different ways is a complex puzzle full of all sorts of challenges."

10

MAE JEMISON

1956–

When Mae Jemison's kindergarten teacher asked her what she wanted to be when she grew up, she replied, "I want to be a scientist." The year was 1961. It was rare for women to work in science, and even more rare for an African-American girl like Mae to succeed. Believing it impossible that Mae could one day be a scientist, her teacher softly asked, "Don't you mean a nurse?" Five-year-old Mae put her small hands on her hips and adamantly repeated herself. "No. I want to be a scientist."

Mae has never focused on limitations, only possibilities. She aimed for the stars, and in 1992 she actually made it there when she became the first African-American woman to go into space!

Mae was born in Decatur, Alabama in 1956, but her parents moved to Chicago when she was three years old. She was a curious child, and in school she would spend hours in the library reading science-fiction novels and looking up scientific facts such as where the earth came from. She loved books that were full of adventure and took place in the future or in space. But much to Mae's frustration, the heroes were usually men. Why couldn't a woman be the one having incredible adventures and traveling through space? Mae turned to an unlikely place to find a role model — the television program Star Trek! One of the crew board the Starship Enterprise was Lieutenant Uhura. Not only was she a woman, but she was also African-American. While not an actual person, to Mae Lieutenant Uhura was an image of what was possible.

Growing up, Mae felt confident that one day she would go into space. To her it wasn't a dream; it was just what was going to happen. "It wasn't whether I wanted to be an astronaut or not; I just wanted to go up there. I thought it was part of our human destiny," she says. So in 1969, when Mae watched astronaut Neil Armstrong take the first steps on

---

☆ Female Firsts in Space ☆

Valentina Tereshkova became the first woman to go into space when she rode aboard the shuttle *Vostok 6* in June of 1963. She spent three days in space and orbited the earth 48 times.

Kathryn D. Sullivan became the first woman to walk in space in October 1984. The American left the space shuttle to demonstrate the refuelling of a satellite.

Eileen Collins became the first woman to command a spaceflight when she led a crew of five aboard the shuttle *Columbia* in 1999.

the moon, she knew that she would be taking her own trip into space as well.

Mae's mother had told her to pay attention to all the adventures she had in life, because in each one there was something to learn that could serve a purpose in the future. Mae followed her mother's advice and was never afraid to do or try anything. She liked dancing and was involved in theater productions at her school. And she worked so hard in high school that she graduated early. She received a *scholarship* and used it to go to Stanford University in California.

Mae was only sixteen when she began at Stanford. Ambitiously, she chose to do two university degrees at the same time, one in African-American studies and one in *chemical engineering*, the field in which chemistry is used to solve technical problems. While at Stanford, she realized that as a woman in science she would be treated differently than a man. She noticed that some of her professors did not see her as a capable scientist. It seemed that women always had to give their best just to be accepted. This was an injustice she hoped she could help eliminate.

After finishing her programs at Stanford in 1977, Mae immediately went to Cornell University Medical College in New York to study to become a doctor. As part of her program, Mae did a very special internship at a refugee camp in Thailand, treating Cambodians who had come to escape the dangers of life in their own country. Working in the emergency room at the camp and running an asthma clinic there, Mae got to help a lot of people.

After finishing at Cornell, Mae wanted a similar experience to the one she had had in Thailand, so she joined the Peace Corps, a program that sends Americans to countries that need aid. In West Africa, where she was sent to work as a doctor, Mae realized that many of the places where she was working did not have access to the types of technology and information that could help the people in those regions. This observation made a deep impression on her.

Once Mae returned to the United States, she worked as a medical doctor, but she hadn't forgotten that childhood ambition to one day travel in space. She took courses in biomedical engineering, a field that looks at how humans deal with being in different environments, like space. And she sent an application to NASA, the National Aeronautics and Space Administration agency, in hopes that she would be chosen as an astronaut.

In 1986, disaster struck NASA. Seconds after the shuttle *Challenger* took off from Cape Canaveral in Florida, it exploded in the sky, killing everyone on board. This terrible tragedy put everything at NASA on hold. NASA wanted to make sure that space exploration was safe and did not involve any unnecessary risks. After a year, NASA felt ready to continue its research. The accident didn't scare Mae off and she re-applied. Out of two thousand applicants, she was one of only fifteen chosen to become part of NASA.

Mae began her long and rigorous astronaut training. To get used to the *weightlessness* she would experience in space, she wore the puffy white astronaut suit, called an extra-vehicular-activity suit, in a large pool of water to see what it felt like to neither float nor sink. She also rode in air-planes that flew in a path similar to a roller coaster's. As the plane flew up and down, up and down, training astronauts got to experience about 20 seconds of weightlessness — not much considering that they would be weightless the entire time they were in space!

Finally, Mae was told the good news — she would be going into space aboard the space shuttle *Endeavour* on mission STS-47. This would be the first joint mission between the United States and Japan, which meant that the shuttle would be carrying American and Japanese astronauts, as well as Spacelab J, a laboratory designed by Japanese scientists. Mae was assigned to be a science mission specialist on the flight. In this important role, she would be conducting experiments aboard the shuttle.

On September 12, 1992, Mae made history as the first African-American woman in space. On the way up, she could see Chicago, the city where she had grown up, and soon she could see the earth itself, the stars and the sun. She recalls, "It was very fulfilling. It was assuring to feel that I belonged anywhere in this universe, whether it was on the earth, or in a star system 10,000 light years away."

Mae took a West African statuette, a Michael Jordan basketball jersey, and a dance poster with her on her trip into space!

The mission lasted 190 hours, and during that time Mae conducted several experiments designed especially for the mission. Many were to see if the lack of *gravity* in space changes the results of normal processes that take place on earth. One of Mae's favorite experiments was observing the growth of frogs. The astronauts had brought frogs to lay eggs in space, and Mae watched as the eggs hatched into tadpoles and grew into frogs. She learned that the frog still went through all the normal stages of growth; that being in space did not change this process.

Mae also got to have some fun on *Endeavour*. She took advantage of her weightlessness to dance on the shuttle, spinning around ten times and taking leaps in which she flew up but never came down.

On September 20, *Endeavour* re-entered the earth's atmosphere. Many people were interested and inspired by

Mae's story, and she happily did many television and newspaper interviews. She wanted people to know that scientists weren't always white men in lab coats. And as a bonus, Mae got to appear on an episode of *Star Trek: The Next Generation*!

Mae loved space travel but in 1993 she decided to leave NASA. She has said that one of the best parts about being a scientist is that "I get to use my creativity. So I get to think about problems and come up with new ideas about how to solve them." With that in mind and building on her past experiences, Mae started The Jemison Group, a company dedicated to using science and technology to help people throughout the world. For example, one of the group's projects is to bring *solar power*, the capacity to use the sun's rays as energy, to areas in Africa where there is a shortage of electricity and plenty of sunlight. These are difficult projects, but Mae feels that her company can make a difference in the world through science.

Mae has taught Environmental Studies at Dartmouth College in New Hampshire, and now lives in Houston, Texas. She also started The Dorothy Jemison Foundation for Excellence, in honor of her mother, who always encouraged her to have so many adventures. Through the foundation, Mae is doing the same for children around the world by running a camp called The Earth We Share. The camp, for children between the ages of twelve and sixteen, encourages what Mae calls "science literacy." She knows that not everyone will become a scientist, but she feels that everyone should be able to understand science because its developments affect all of us.

Mae is fluent in several languages — besides English, she speaks Russian, Japanese and Swahili!

Mae has received many honors for her

achievements, including being inducted into the National Women's Hall of Fame and receiving several honorary doctorate degrees. Her adventures will continue, though — the universe is a big place!

GLOSSARY

Ammonites: The spiral-shaped fossil of the extinct species Ammonoidea, from the Devonian period (about 410 to 360 million years ago) to the Cretaceous period (about 140 to 65 million years ago) in geologic time.

Anthropology: The branch of science that studies human beings, including their origins, physical development and culture, and how they differ from other animals.

Astrolabe: An instrument used in astronomy and navigation for measuring the altitude of the sun or stars.

Atom: Made up of a nucleus that holds neutrons and protons and is surrounded by electrons, it is the smallest component of an element that still has the chemical properties of that element.

Atomic bomb: A powerful weapon whose explosive force is caused when the nucleus of an atom is split and an abundance of energy is released.

Beta decay: A process that occurs in radioactive atoms that causes changes to take place inside the nucleus and affects the atomic weight of the element.

Bachelor's degree: The first degree a person can earn from a college or university for completing the necessary courses.

Biology: The branch of science that deals with all living things.

Biomedical engineering: A field of engineering that investigates and designs solutions to medical and biological problems, such as artificial limbs and organs.

Chemical engineering: The science of designing and producing chemicals, generally for industrial uses.

Chemistry: The study of elements and their characteristics, the results of combining them, and how they behave under certain conditions.

Compound: In chemistry, a substance that is composed of two or more elements, for example water, which is made up of two hydrogen atoms and one oxygen atom.

Conservation: The act of protecting and preserving rivers, forests, wildlife and other natural resources to prevent their disappearance.

Conservation of parity: A principle in physics recognizing an innate symmetry in nature. It was thought that every process in science will behave the same as its mirror image would. This principle has been very important in atomic and nuclear physics, and it was discovered that conservation of parity does not always occur in certain nuclear reactions.

Data: Factual information, specially organized for analysis, such as values obtained from a scientific experiment.

DDT: Short for dichlorodiphenyltrichloroethane, a chemical used to kill insects that destroy crops. It has been prohibited in Canada since 1969 and in the United States since 1973.

Dinosauria: The Greek word for dinosaurs — large, extinct reptiles that lived about 250 to 100 million years ago.

Dissertation: A very long essay on a particular subject written by a student to qualify for a doctoral degree (Ph.D.).

Double helix: The spiral arrangement that forms the structure of DNA.

DNA: Short for deoxyribonucleic acid, the material that transfers genetic characteristics from parents to children in all life forms.

Eclipse: The blocking of the light of the moon or sun caused when the earth, moon and sun become aligned in a particular way.

Ecology: Related to biology, it is the study of the relationships of living things to their physical environment and to one another.

Electron: A tiny particle that has a negative charge and circles the nucleus.

Element: A substance that cannot be further broken down without losing its characteristic properties, for example hydrogen.

Emanation: An emission released by a source. The term is now outdated and no longer used in science.

Engineering: The application of science to practical ends, for example designing, building and operating structures, machines or systems.

Environment: In ecology, the air, water, minerals, organisms and all other external factors that surround and affect a living thing at any time.

Evolution: The theory that all living things developed from earlier forms through gradual changes made to adapt to an environment.

Experiment: A test designed to discover something unknown or to prove that a theory is either correct or incorrect.

Fieldwork: Work done on a site, rather than just in a laboratory, in order to collect data through research, exploration and direct observation.

Fossil: The preserved remains or imprints of living things that date back to prehistoric times.

Gene: A segment of DNA, the unit that carries a particular hereditary trait.

Geologic time: The extremely long time covering the physical formation and development of the earth, or the earth's geologic history. Geologic time is divided into several periods of millions of years each.

Geology: A branch of science that looks at the rocks that form the earth and the changes they have undergone through history.

Geyser: A hot spring that periodically sends up fountain-like jets of water and steam into the air.

Gravity: A natural force that attracts objects toward the center of the earth.

Habituation: The process of making a particular situation familiar. An example is when wild animals become used to having humans around and behave differently as a result.

Hydroscope: A device used for viewing objects below the surface of water.

Ichthyosaur: An extinct fish-like marine reptile that ranged from 1.2 to 12 meters in length with a round body, a large head, bulging eyes and four flippers.

Jurassic period: A geologic period that occurred from about 208 to 146 million years ago and was characterized by an abundance of dinosaurs.

Lava: The molten rock that exits a volcano during an eruption in liquid form.

Law of nature: An expression used to refer to a set of rules always known to be true in nature and that are scientifically proven.

Magma: Melted rock that exists beneath or within the earth's crust.

Master's degree: A degree awarded by a university to a person who has a bachelor's degree and has completed the requirements in a particular field of study.

Microscope: An instrument that increases the visual size of an object.

Neutron: A particle that forms part of the nucleus of an atom and has neither a positive nor a negative charge.

Nuclear energy: The energy that is stored in the nucleus of an atom and that can be released through different procedures.

Nuclear physics: A branch of physics that studies the components, structure and behavior of the nucleus of an atom.

Nuclear shell model: A model of the structure of the nucleus of an atom, describing it as being constructed of several layers or shells in which protons and neutrons spin in orbit.

Nucleus: The central core of an atom that is composed of neutrons and protons.

Observation: A method of collecting data by viewing or noting a fact or occurrence over a period of time for a scientific purpose.

Paleontology: A branch of geology that studies forms of life that existed in former geologic periods, as represented by their fossils.

Pesticides: Chemical products that are used to kill plants or animals and that are harmful to people.

Periodic table: A chart that organizes all known elements according to their characteristics.

Ph.D. (Doctor of Philosophy): Also called a doctorate, a Ph.D. is one of several kinds of doctoral degrees. A doctorate is the highest degree awarded by a university to a person who has completed an accepted dissertation in a particular field of study.

Philosophy: The study of the truths and principles underlying knowledge, or of the most general causes and principles of the universe.

Physics: The branch of science that deals with matter and energy and their interactions.

Plesiosaur: A large, extinct marine reptile that had paddle-like limbs and lived about 250 to 100 million years ago.

Pterodactylus Macronyx: A type of flying reptile from the Jurassic (about 208 to 146 million years ago) and Cretaceous (about 140 to 65 million years ago) periods, which had a small tail and a birdlike beak.

Proton: A tiny particle with a positive charge found in the nucleus of an atom.

Pyroclastic flow: A mix of gas, ash, and rock that exits a volcano during eruption.

Quantum mechanics: A branch of physics that studies the forces and motion occurring in atoms, molecules, and other physical systems.

Radioactivity: A property of certain elements in which the spontaneous emission of a particle results from changes in the nucleus of the atom.

Radiation: The process by which energy is emitted as particles or waves.

Radium: A highly radioactive metallic element that produces radon gas.

Radon: A radioactive chemical element that comes in the form of a gas and is derived from the element radium.

Scholarship: A sum of money or other aid granted to a student for displaying outstanding merit so she or he can pursue academic studies.

Solar power: The energy that is given off by the sun.

Spin-orbit coupling: A theory used to explain the motion and interactions of protons and neutrons in the nuclear shell model of the atom.

Squaloraja: A prehistoric fish related to sharks and rays.

Theory: A proposed explanation that becomes accepted once it has been tested and proven scientifically.

Thesis: An essay on a particular subject on which a person has done original research; written in order to earn a diploma or degree.

Transmutation: The conversion of one chemical element into another.

Volcano: An opening in the earth's crust through which molten rock and steam are expelled. The word is also used to mean the mountain or hill caused by an eruption.

Volcanologist: A scientist who studies volcanoes.

Weightlessness: The state that occurs when the effects of gravity have been removed.

X-ray crystallography: A technique used to determine the structure of a crystal.

Zoology: A branch of biology that studies animal life.

Sources

Hypatia

Dzielska, Maria. *Hypatia of Alexandria*. Cambridge, Massachusetts: Harvard University Press, 1995.

Ogilvie, Marilyn Bailey. *Women in Science: Antiquity through the Nineteenth Century*. Cambridge, Massachusetts: Massachusetts Institute of Technology Press,1988.

Fideler, David. *Alexandria 2: The Journal of the Western Cosmological Traditions*. Grand Rapids, Michigan: Phanes Press, 1994.

http://www.polyamory.org/~howard/Hypatia/Hubbard_19 28.html

http://www.polyamory.org/~howard/Hypatia/Mangasarian.html

http://www-groups.dcs.st-and.ac.uk:80/~history/ Mathematicians/Hypatia.html

http://www.astr.ua.edu/4000WS/HYPATIA.html

Mary Anning

Torrens, Hugh. "Mary Anning of Lyme; 'the greatest fossilist the world ever knew.'" *British Journal of the History of Science*. 28 (1995): 257 – 284.

http:// www.ucmp.berkeley.edu/history/anning.html

http://www.lymeregismuseum.co.uk/fossils.htm

http://www.lymeregis.net/pages/maryann.html

http://www.rowfant.demon.co.uk/maryanning.htm

Harriet Brooks Pitcher

Black, Harry. *Canadian Scientists and Inventors*. Markham, Ontario: Pembroke Publishers Ltd., 1997.

Rayner-Canham, Geoffrey, and Marelene Rayner-Canham. *Harriet Brooks: Pioneer Nuclear Physicist*. Montreal: McGill-Queen's University Press, 1992.

http://www.physics.ucla.edu/~cwp/Phase2/ Brooks,_Harriet@842580299.html

http://www.aip.org/history/curie/unstable.htm

http://www.rutherford.org.nz/biography.htm

Maria Goeppert-Mayer

McGrayne, Sharon Bertsch. *Nobel Prize Women: Their Lives, Struggles and Momentous Discoveries*. Secaucus, New Jersey: Carol Publishing Group, 1993.

Stille, Darlene. *Extraordinary Women Scientists*. Chicago: Children's Press, 1995.

http://www.physics.ucla.edu/~moszkows/mgm/mgmhmpg.htm

Rachel Carson

Lear, Linda. *Rachel Carson: Witness for Nature*. New York: Henry Holt and Company, 1997.

Stille, Darlene. *Extraordinary Women Scientists*. Chicago: Children's Press, 1995.

http://www.ecotopia.org/ehof/carson/bio.html

http://clinton2.nara.gov/WH/EOP/OVP/24hours/carson.html

Chien-Shiung Wu

McGrayne, Sharon Bertsch. *Nobel Prize Women: Their Lives, Struggles and Momentous Discoveries*. Secaucus, New Jersey: Carol Publishing Group, 1993.

Stille, Darlene. *Extraordinary Women Scientists*. Chicago: Children's Press, 1995.

http://www.columbia.edu/cu/record/archives/vol22/vol22_iss15/record2215.16.html

http://www.physics.hku.hk/~tboyce/ss/topics/women/ascent.html

http://www.chinanah.com/liuhe/wujianxion.htm

http://www.physics.ucla.edu/~cwp/articles/wuobit.html

Rosalind Franklin

Sayre, Anne. *Rosalind Franklin and DNA*. New York: W.W. Norton and Company Inc., 2000.

Stille, Darlene. *Extraordinary Women Scientists*. Chicago: Children's Press, 1995.

http://www.physics.ucla.edu/~cwp/articles/franklin/piper.html

Biruté Galdikas

Galdikas, Biruté. *Reflections of Eden*. Toronto: Little, Brown and Company, 1995.

http://www.borneo.com.au/kalimantan/campleakey.htm

http://www.discovery.com/stories/nature/orangs/leakey.html

http://www.science.ca/scientists/scientistprofile.php?pID=7

http://www.orangutan.org/home/home.php

Catherine Hickson

Personal correspondence with Dr. Hickson.

Wood, Daniel. "Waiting For Another Blast." *Canadian Geographic* (May-June 1993), pp. 28-30.

http://www.nrcan.gc.ca

http://www.discoverlearning.com/scienceworks/profiles/ catherine_hickson.html

http://www.science.uwaterloo.ca/earth/geoscience/hickson.html

http://volcano.und.nodak.edu/vw.html

http://vulcan.wr.usgs.gov/LivingWith/VolcanicFacts/ misc_volcanic_facts.html#vulcan

http://news.bbc.co.uk/cbbcnews/hi/find_out/guides/ tech/volcanoes/newsid_1768000/1768629.stm

Mae Jemison

Stille, Darlene. *Extraordinary Women Scientists*. Chicago: Children's Press, 1995.

http://www.maejemison.com/

http://quest.arc.nasa.gov/space/frontiers/jemison.html

http://www.pbs.org/newshour/bb/science/july-dec99/ apollo_7-20.html

http://www.quest.arc.nasa.gov/women/TODTWD/ jemison.bio.html

http://www.stanford.edu/dept/news/stanfordtoday/ed/ 9607/9607mj01.shtml

http://www.webswithwings.com/wcc/heroines/mae.html

http://teacher.scholastic.com/space/mae_jemison/index.htm

http://programs.researchchannel.com/displayseries.asp? collid=266

SOURCES

Other helpful sites:

http://www.astr.ua.edu/4000WS/

http://www.factmonster.com/

http://www.howstuffworks.com/

http://www.britannica.com/

http://www.oup.co.uk/oxed/children/yoes/sites/general/

http://www-nsd.lbl.gov/LBLPrograms/nsd/education/ABC/
wallchart/guide.html

http://www.sciencemuseum.org.uk/on-line/index.asp

http://www.pbs.org/wgbh/aso/

PHOTO CREDITS